**Date: 11/22/21**

# It Is Hot

BY TORA STEPHENCHEL

It is hot
and the sun
is shining.

It is hot
so we find
some shade.

It is hot
so we drink
lemonade.

It is hot
so we go
to the pool.

It is hot
so we jump
in the water.

It is hot
so we splash.

It is hot
and we play.

It is hot
and we splash
some more.

It is hot
and the water
cools us.

It is hot
but we have fun!

## Note to Caregivers and Educators

Sight words are a foundation for reading. It's important for young readers to have sight words memorized at a glance without breaking them down into individual letter sounds. Sight words are often phonetically irregular and can't be sounded out, so readers need to memorize them. Knowing sight words allows readers to focus on more difficult words in the text. The intent of this book is to repeat specific sight words as many times as possible throughout the story. Through repetition of the words, emerging readers will recognize, and ideally memorize, each sight word. Memorizing sight words can help improve readers' literacy skills.

hot

is

it

## About the Author

Tora Stephenchel lives in Minnesota. She loves to spend time with her son, daughter, husband, and two silly dogs.

Published by The Child's World®
1980 Lookout Drive • Mankato, MN 56003-1705
800-599-READ • www.childsworld.com

Photographs © 3445128471/Shutterstock.com: 6; altanaka/Shutterstock.com: 13; Anna Komissarenko/Shutterstock.com: 9; legenda/Shutterstock.com.10; Pixel-Shot/Shutterstock.com: 23; sakkmesterke/Shutterstock.com: cover, 1; sergio victor vega/Shutterstock.com: 14, 21; T. Kimmeskamp/Shutterstock.com: 5; TY Lim/Shutterstock.com: 17; Wolfgang Filser/Shutterstock.com: 2; YanLev/Shutterstock.com: 18

ISBN 9781503845046 (Reinforced Library Binding)
ISBN 9781503846555 (Portable Document Format)
ISBN 9781503847743 (Online Multi-user eBook)
LCCN 2020931118

Printed in the United States of America